The Song of the Grackle

D1379450

The Song of the Grackle

Mattie McClane

Myrtle Hedge Press

Copyright © 2019 by Myrtle Hedge Press, Kure Beach NC
All rights reserved
Printed in the United States of America

ISBN: 978-0-9722466-9-9
Library of Congress Control Number: 2019900806

Design and layout by
        Val Sherer, Personalized Publishing Services
ID 41063361 © Redwood8 | Dreamstime.com
ID 23729991 © Gilles Malo | Dreamstime.com

To Leslie Dupree and John C. Beydler

The Song of the
Grackle

❧ I ❧

I hear a distant voice
that sounds like crickets
rubbing
their legs together
or ocean waves
throwing foam
at high tide.

Mattie McClane

It speaks to me.
It says move
from windy
and wet September
when roofs fly
from houses
and the president
is doing a public relations act.
The call once told me
to follow
a bright star
and hide out
in barns
at evening meet friendly neighbors
who shared the values
of freedom.
It speaks
to me about liberty

The Song of the Grackle

cut chains put
on by a master
many masters
or whoever owns
the land
the jet planes tanks
that can't be
in the big parade
because they tear
up streets.
The voice cries
it commands
it says march
to even ballerinas
in contemporary choreography
downtown Los Angeles
or cultural hubs
in the middle of pancake flatlands

it tells me
to put tennis shoes
on swoosh three stripes
lace tightly
then step on hardwood floors
where the sea
is only blocks away
the river
is a two-day drive
past cornfields
the dirt is black
productive
making farmers rich
on paper. The noise sounds
like a tractor running
turning soil
in measured rows
after people came

from Sweden
with two pairs
of pants, a coat
to go into the coal mines
or to plow
the owners'
land with horses
the pictures
in black and white
of men
with cough drop
brothers' beards
the clear instruction
is to leave all
that is comfortable
scenic for the sake
of release
from would-be despots

who scapegoat
the weak
and disconnected
the country quilt-maker
who takes fabric squares
into a warm design
a mix of colors
a mix of people
no longer free.

The woman sits
in an office
the sounds of traffic
from a city
where the poor stand out
on street corners
knocking on car windows
asking for change.

The coffers
are empty drivers
are broke
paying bills online
until they
are penniless
The sound of tires
of speed
the race
of rush hour
sounding
against barrier walls
say move leave
travel down
the highway
to a grassy meadow
far from the rats
that tease

outdoor felines
from a place where
the taxes are high
and the water
is poison
with lead
aging infrastructure
the roads
crumble
except
the tar one
smooth bubbling
impressionable
oily iridescent soles
the black can only
be removed
with lighter fluid
that is past

The Song of the Grackle

and everybody knows
it. No more Pall Mall
diseased lungs
for carpet-layers
and Singer sewing machine
salesmen
now long gone
the voice came in like
pine needles sweeping
the wind.
It is time
to get out
or before I know it
no one
will believe in
anything
higher
than a party's platform

with balloons
confetti distractions.
Can I walk away?
Can you depart?
The words say clearly
that the shoes
are worn
but must go
they've been places
to horse fields
in Kentucky
to Rocky Mountains
where hummingbirds
drink grenadine
to a land joined
by rivers
and separated
by governmental borders

The Song of the Grackle

to coastal communities
where dogs
are not allowed
on the beach strand.

The desire to move
hasn't left me.
I hear the bells
from the university peal
they say get on
from landmark buildings
to a view
of Old Main
of the Mississippi
of the water, always
flowing
around
a fallen tree

making its way
with the current
pools swirling
around jutting
branches.
I always come home
I have roots
like a poplar
knobby wooden arms
extending down
the shiny mud banks meeting
the wide stream.

I dream of pilgrims
the voyagers
who wanted religious freedom
independence
the right to believe

walk for rights
to be unbound
to imagine democracy
in place
move step high
journey
into the night
looking at the sky
your star cosmic
and full
of destiny. Join
the voices
the beginning
of choirs
with sopranos
alto
tenor
and bass

booming
at traffic stops
being heard
at noisy rabbles
for festive audiences
in the quiet homes
where the elderly couple live
on Social Security
in churches
when the congregation
has gone
went about
daily routines
I dream this,
that democracy
will hold
in a nation
that thinks

on its own
and the truth
is sacred.

Move for the love
of children
restless
fidgety
crying
unsuspecting heirs
when scientists issue
their reports
about man-made
climate change
they were taught
to deny
to ignore
to fabricate

and are expected now
to solve problems.
They will
want to step
away from
wildfires
droughts
floods
they will be
a displaced people
who will want
to go home
wanting rootedness.

The country
is not your own.
Be on your way.
Yesterday's flag

was to fight
and die
for don't tread
on me
or make
me believe
in causes, causes
are lost. Put on
tawny leather boots
to the calves
to walk miles in
go quickly
through dense forests
across chilly deserts
through meadow lanes
to town hall
city streets
like forbearers

who believed
in the right
of people to live
in harmony
after a contest
the better wins
in faraway wars
suspended rifles
and bayonets
peace comes
from battles legs
are amputated
from running at
a fortified fence
the rubber tires burn
are purposely
set on fire
smoke

The Song of the Grackle

blackening
obscuring
the air
the sight
the target
the enlisted
one hears
the cries say
move on, take
what is left
of principle
and call
your mother
she will
not answer
the years
have passed
she is no longer young

and victorious
the government paycheck
still covers bills
for the kid's
dental work
for fuel oil
long after
the conviction
the reason
the people
left mourning.

New Zealand's
celebrated citizen
breaks away
from the father
the local patriarch
in Wellington

society get-togethers
satin dresses
a changed name
Katherine Mansfield
the rebel
who travels
to London
and will marry
a critic. The past
is scandalous
the future
more promising
no regrets
praise
to a maternal
grandmother
childhoods spent
at the beach

with little voices
the visual made alive
with words
the feeling of bliss
the moon shining
on the pear tree
the claimed sexuality
then a beloved
brother killed
in the service
the girl known
in her own right
for stories
She 'd move
to the country
for cures
tending cows
spotted wings

The Song of the Grackle

with tuberculosis
with a guru
a health advisor
the march complete
at a very young age

The life stayed
in my mind
a literary outsider
with Woolf
the crazy woman
the only one now
certain to be
in the canon
a female wonder
someone
to dream of being like
the humor

the seriousness
the gossip
of Bloomsbury
retold in diaries
March for sanity
for a woman's genius
one half woman
the other half
necessary
to create
wholeness
incandescence
a Times review
a curious trip
to Haworth
to see
Bronte's small shoes
traveling

to Brussels
walk to our mothers
march to them
with a glued spine
in paperback
in an electronic format
the old man
outlives
his children
and shoots the sky
in a churchyard at night.

❧ II ❧

Go when you can.
Pray they don't find gold
on ancestral lands
profiteers
government officials
will move tribes
the strong
the now hearty

the elderly
the sick
will be relocated.
Others can dig deep
into the earth
and pull
out cash
for ornate buggies
ten room houses
the familiarity
the culture
is lost
displaced
as a whole people
walk cross
state lines
to a reserve special
the chief

is replaced
with a governor
a warrior marries
a woman
of German stock.
It must be said.
I say it.
Take another way
for past injustice
the dust
of the moccasin
it rises
it chokes
it dirties
around steps
from Georgia
to Oklahoma. Do
not forget

what good men
will do for money
the tears do
not belong
to community leaders
talking compassion
give reasons spin
the truth.
Greedy people
officials
explaining cruelty
to a weary public
who always want
to believe
in best intentions,
who want
not to be
bothered
or become involved.

The potato crop fails
the Great Hunger
a million people starve
a million leave
their homes.
The plants' leaves turn black
like corpses
from a blight
but the citizens
foolishly
export food
nourishment
sweet butter
to the landowners
who sit
in legislatures
and pass laws
to benefit the few.

The body
grows weak
is susceptible to illness
What offence
do the poor commit
to watch loved ones die
wither away
waste? Where
is the mercy
of God
when one
is forced
to march, to leave
the graves
of ancestors
and the newly dead?

Go on, lift the legs
find a better circumstance
Do not wait
to be forced
when nobody hears
the ballot is pale
shadowy cold
like Northern sunlight
the election
is rigged
votes uncounted
and the heart
bursts with sentiment
against oppressors
wearing wingtips
pin-striped suits

the hegemony
of privilege
of connection
of networks
of silk
of gold
of fossil fuels pumping
in the neighbor's yard.
Speak now
the mechanical see-saw
or the tunnels
for coal burnt
in the open air
tower-like clouds
toxic thunderheads
red hot bituminous rocks cooled
in a lake
tainted fish

The Song of the Grackle

selenium, mercury
where people
play water sports
and drink beer.

I can talk of nicer things
but my eye
is on the light
my ear
on the voice
It reminds me
of a kinder place
where supper
is served to all people
the laughter
of ordinary folks
who work
in the factories

for 20 years
and name their children
after handsome
and popular
TV celebrities.

 **III**

I walk
by roses
and wonder why
they open
as full as frosted rolls
when planted
in the garden.

Everything beautiful
calls out
to stand up
to witness
to not let ugliness
go unmentioned.
A star ray guides me.
It makes me think
of the others
when the world
was unbearable
causing sufferers
to carry through,
to keep walking
to carry the cross
My knowledge
of footpaths
of trails

of gravel roads
will help find
where freedom
abounds.

I hear the chimes
of clocktowers
and the hands
are moving
like my legs across
stony ways.

I search through
memories
my stories
that instruct
biographies
of heroines

and saints
the earth's womb
speaks to me.

I have heard
of the wise
doctors of philosophy
professors
theologians
St. Teresa Benedicta of the Cross
who died
at the orders
of sinful men.
Do you see
this era
with its pervasive lies
and self-serving notables?
The sound says march.

I heard of a woman
who led an army
a young leader
professing her Grace
she was called
a heretic
a witch
for her military prowess.
I heard of a man
who believed in Truth
who led
a rebel movement
spontaneous
participants
for hours
for days
people
would walk

to make salt
from the ocean
to gain national
independence
nonviolent
resistance
the actions
that brought low
British rulers
who hoarded power.
The sea is listening
and talking.

This is the song
of the grackle.
Its chatter and clicks
are annoying
to the songbird

and painted bunting
It is not for the extraordinary
the celebrated
the coveted. It
is a song
that sounds pretty
to a common beach
bird brown
and shiny black
with an open beak
and yellow eyes.
Its song
is for everyone
discounted
poor and hard
to love.
The noisy fuss
in the middle

of grassy dunes
and sea oats
must say march
in a resonating pitch
for waitresses
the postman
the elevator mechanic
the window cleaner
the custodian
the sanitation worker
to whoever else
is unheard.
It's a song
that cannot
be denied or forgotten
It is a lovely song
to its kind.
The grackle loves

the grackle's tune.

It says move, march
over the bridge
at Selma
with troopers
present. Never
forget the 30-something man
with a gift
for oratory
for wisdom
and courage
who inspired people
to walk
to forbidden places
to demand
a say
a ballot

when there

was anger

in the dominant heart.

Forgive

the brutality

of clubs

of shouts

of curses

when people

don't love

as they should

imagining

the robbery

of good things

too much scarcity

the other

is the night's thief.

The Song of the Grackle

I have heard
of a time
when women
couldn't practice law
when they
did research
in the backroom.
Their voices
never rose
in courtrooms.

My great-grandmother
couldn't vote
when she turned 21.
She took photographs
of her brothers
in doughboy uniforms

they were off
to a war
in which
she had no say. I turn
the album's pages
and I say step
for every
girl child
who realized
few dreams.

My father broke lamps
to get my mother's attention
to announce
his displeasure
They were expensive
gold-toned
with crystal

But he didn't think
she heard him.

The politicians shock
with their words.
Some thought
equality
was written
in stone
like settled law. Take
to the open
young women
without
generations
of wealth
or financial
backers.
Or those people

who were packed
into ships
to middle passage
the advantage
is slippery
uncertain
a gambler's bet
an era can take
it away.

Abigail Adams
knew about
the desire
for power.
It never relents.
It is never
satisfied
and it is not given

up without
struggle people
do not rest
swing the legs
to the side
of the bed
awaken
my friend
from slumber
put them
on the hard ground
open the door
and walk in crowds.

Thousands
of black birds
take off
to pepper

the late summer sky,
airy ribbons twisting
turning
the migration
a spectacle
the move
to ample food
Let us go
like a flock
or a thunderous herd
staying together.
Who knows
what can happen?
I am reminded
of a sea
that opened
to a people.
I am reminded

The Song of the Grackle

of the women
who badgered
their husbands
at dinnertime
disobeying
the rules
of proper ladies.

The fertile minds
at universities
argue theories
aren't restrained.
I believe
in the force
of notions
of books
of science
of conclusion

something higher
than rhetoric
only meant
to persuade.

Advertising worlds
will relent
the agenda
won't be
about profit
silk-pocketed men
will go home
to spend time
with families.

The light appeals to me
The voice whispers
in my ear

to move
keep going
the many
in unison
like a hundred slaves
who made a pact
not to be put down
in chains
in shackles
but to seek a place
where all could be heard
in the daylight
with a hundred light
points cast
on the walls
the brilliant sunshine.
revealed.

∾ **IV** ∾

This is the house of light
with windows
in every direction
it enfolds me
uncovers me
emboldens

with its spirit gained
from churches
from a gift rosary.
I have said
my prayers
the commandment
is to step
people come out
from what binds
walk in pairs
or the footprints
of thousands
marking the road
a footpath
when the clouds rain

when they
do not rain
and dust rises

around soles
the movement
of grackles
through the sky
of revolutionaries
of rebels
of the ordinary
who want what
is better
more truth
more facts
a free press
more democracy
more justice
in a failing world.

I can talk
of happier times

a child is born

emerges

the pain stops

with naming. Give

the sentiment

a word

a meaning

an introduction

something

to be called

from infancy

recognition

the baptismal water

of beginnings

of schooling

of higher degrees

worked on

for a decade.

The Song of the Grackle

Who will say?
Who will listen?
Who will care?
The right words
will be spoken
are waited
for like an Atlantic
waterwheel
pushing itself
with energy
natural force
expelling
seven lucky
dolphins
that swim
in the rushing
the retreating spray
near granite rock.

My ear hears
words following words.

I have heard
of a woman
who lived among
the poor
asking for nothing
but the approval
of God
nursing
the lesions
of unloved humanity.
They called
her holy
because caring
is an extraordinary effort
that is empathy

that is compassion
when others
can't see it.
The crowd does
not roar
or applaud
a lack
of self interest
the buying season
is extended
from October
to December time
to spend
to buy gifts
to part
with cash
for the hiring
of part-time

workers
who are without benefits
or a vacation
to a tropical island
or a motel deep
in the mountains
of Tennessee.

The hero's
heart pumps fast
it anticipates
the danger
of drought
of high temperatures
to structures.
The inferno
is stoked
by Santa Ana winds

The Song of the Grackle

it descends
it engulfs
leaving no trace
of blueprints' design
of best dreams.

People flee
they march
to a safer existence.
A warning goes
out. Take notice
that the earth
has limits
is restricted
in the amount
of abuse
it can take.
The sirens' sound

repeatedly
then are over.
A planet means business,
and people
will act differently
or die.

I have heard
of a man
who wanted
to be alone
and lived
by a pond, chronicling
the natural world
The man didn't pay
his taxes,
couldn't support
an unjust war.

He went
to jail maybe
a star ray led him
or he heard
the call
that is in my mind.
It takes
into account
that daffodils
bloom
in clusters
after being alone.

The idea will grow
it will prompt
the grackle
to fly where
the summer

and winter
are sustainable, looking
to be vital
for the next year.
A chocolate
chip sky stirred
in the white air,
mass movement
the sight
of a higher will.

This is the song
of the grackle,
or the house
of light
the scent
of clover
in a Midwestern field

the light purple
flowers
that are sweet
to the taste.
They call the bees
and grazing animals
that depend
on open land.
Walk outside
from low
or tall
buildings
down
stairs one step
after another
keep a pace
but find patience
deliberation

resolve.
Find the reason
to move
to travel
a days' drive
in the sound
of the wind
lightly blowing
small columbines
or the Indian paintbrush
on a hikers' trail.

I hear the voice
in the rustling aspens
in a rush
of mountain air
wind chimes tinkle
and the broken rock popping

under tires
on the road
on the shoulder
of winding turns
the message '
comes up
silently now
through the chest
a repetition
a strong suggestion.
I listen intently
to coursing utterances
quietly spoken
in the body
in cutting sensation
to the center
to the mind.
It is emphatic

will not be ignored.
I ask to hear again
the talk between chatty angels
and falling stars
the noise
they must make
to enter
the atmosphere
still quite fiery
making onlookers wonder
if the sound
if the sight
can be counted on.

The Song of the Grackle

 **V**

If a tree falls in the forest
does it say march
move for brothers
and the sisters
who taught
at Catholic colleges

for 30 years
and decided
they loved women?
When one
is alone
outside
of tradition
of institutions
of creeds
and everything
that upholds patriarchy
the sound
the light
the migration
will seem reasonable.

Go now others
will follow

shake off expectations
assumptions
or facts
that deal in the flesh.
Leave the past
its nightmares
the fathers
who never buy
dog food products
for a bloated mongrel
that is hidden
that is loved
that is dying
in the attic
in walk-ins
the caves
kept in houses.

Unhand me
memories
moving pictures
it releases me
from the bondage
of oppressors
who want
their way
in the home
with thermostats
with light switches
in the church
in politics. I say
again, I will be free
and will loosen
the fetters
of others.

∾ **VI** ∾

A new tender plant
will grow
from a field
of ashes.
The earth

will cool
from its fever
on the day
everyone hears
the fluttering
of feathers
of bird wings
the prophecy
of the grackle
that is not
so pretty
to witnesses
without shiny tailfeathers.

I have heard
of an art critic
who retold the story
of the vineyard

The Song of the Grackle

the workers
who went in late
and were paid
the same.
"The only wealth
is life," the life
of power-brokers
who give
to campaigns
to universities
and those beggars
who stand
in intersections
holding signs. They say,
I am hungry
I am without
the famine
is with us

until the buds
are fresh, new
and reappear
on the smoldering trees.

History might save
the world
protect it
from those given power
who ignore
disregard
the well-being
of thousands.
Certainly, they fall
like statues
the memorialized
who are no
longer chic

pulled forward
to the hard ground.

The collective brain
that keeps liberty
is tucked away
in the vault
firing synapses
when necessary
about how far
we've come
from forgiving
atrocities
the canisters
that go off
on the border
the children crying
or squirming

in the sanctuary
standing
on shoulders
to see consecrated bread.

I will depend on the mythos
the pattern
of people's minds
the psychology
of masses
of folks
to discern
that which favors
freedom.
The song
of the grackle
becomes loud,
present

calling listeners

to move

to step

to dance

to walk

to its common tune.

The fields

will turn green

with crops

that feed

the hungry.

The land

will bear fruit

trees heavy

with plums

or apples.

The star's fire

will give light

showing off
the dark night's path.
The bird
will take flight
over the seeded earth.

Come to the bountiful table
that stretches
across every
comet-streaked sky
with roasted meats
with warm breads
no more scapegoats
or guilty people
pass the baskets
of plenty. See
the morning river.

March, you
are welcomed home.

About The Author

Mattie McClane (Kristine A. Kaiser) is an American novelist, poet, and journalist. She is the second and youngest daughter born to James L. and Shirlie I. Myers in Moline, Illinois. Her father was a commercial artist and her mother worked as a secretary.

McClane's earliest education was in the Catholic schools. Her experience with their teachings deeply affected her. At a young age, she became aware of gender inequality. She credits her early religious instruction for making her think about "all kinds of truths" and ethical matters.

McClane's parents divorced when she was eight years old. Her mother remarried attorney John G. Ames and the new couple moved to a house beside the Rock River. The river centrally figures in McClane's creative imagination. She describes her childhood as being "extraordinarily free and close to nature."

McClane moved to Colorado and married John Kaiser

in 1979, in Aurora, just East of Denver.

They then moved to Bettendorf, Iowa where they had three children. John worked as a chemist. Mattie became interested in politics, joining the local League of Women Voters. According to McClane, she spent her 20s "caring for young children and working for good government."

She graduated from Augustana College with a B.A. degree in the Humanities. She began writing a political column for Quad-Cities Online and Small Newspaper Group, based in Illinois.

Her family moved to Louisville, Kentucky where she continued with her journalism and then earned an M.A. in English from the University of Louisville. Critically acclaimed author Sena Jeter Naslund directed her first creative thesis, "Unbuttoning Light and Other Stories," which was later published in a collection.

She was accepted to the University of North Carolina at Wilmington's M.F.A. in Creative Writing Program, where she wrote the short novel Night Ship, working under the tutelage of Pulitzer Prize winning author Alison Lurie. McClane studied with Dennis Sampson in poetry also. She graduated in 1999.

She would write a column for the High Point Enterprise in North Carolina. She would later write for the News and Observer. McClane has regularly published commentary for over 25 years.

Mattie McClane is the author of *Night Ship: A Voyage*

of Discovery (2003), *River Hymn: Essays Evangelical and Political* (2004), *Wen Wilson* (2009), *Unbuttoning Light: The Collected Short Stories of Mattie McClane* (2012), *Now Time* (2013), *Stations of the Cross* (2016), *The Mother Word: An Exploration of the Visual* (2017), and *Simeon's Canticle* (2018).

She lives in North Carolina.